Healthy Heather

and Her Magic Fruits and Vegetables

A Book about Kids' Nutrition, Kindness, and
Celebrating Individuality

By Dr. Kristen Poe

Book formatted by Bluebobo

This book is dedicated to my loving family and friends, but especially FDP, GG, VIP, and MVP.

You are truly my inspiration, the loves of my life, and my "why" in everything I do. You are my greatest blessings and I love you.

This is the story of Healthy Heather and her magic fruits and vegetables. Although she looked ordinary, Heather was actually a very extraordinary girl.

Some of her favorite things to do were gymnastics and yoga with her mom and dad and twin sisters and brother, reading books, and learning new things at school. Her classmates were all amazed at how smart she was. In fact, she was the smartest kid in school! She loved going to school!

However, most of all she loved eating vegetables and fruits. Every chance Heather had, she would eat yummy fruits and vegetables. In fact, when she ate all of her fruits and vegetables, especially green vegetables, she got super special powers. She especially loved to eat spinach, broccoli, carrots, and blueberries.

When she ate her fruits and vegetables, she grew very strong and could turn into a superhero with her magical powers. She could jump so high that she could reach the top of a tree. She could lift a car or a huge rock over her head. She could run like lighting, and she could solve math problems and read books in less than one minute. She got straight A's in school.

Only Heather's parents knew about her special superhero powers. They made sure to let her know how special and wonderful she was each day. But none of her classmates at school knew about her special powers. In fact, Heather was a small girl! However, she knew as soon as she ate her fruits and vegetables, she would turn into a brainiac superhero.

Every day, during snack time at school, Heather would have a big bowl of green vegetables and berries. She loved snack time because it gave her a lot of energy. It helped her learn and get good grades. Her fruits and vegetables also gave her secret special powers and kept her healthy.

However, Healthy Heather had a classmate named Billy the Bully who would tease her every day about her healthy snacks and lunches.

Billy the Bully was a lot bigger than Heather and would say, "Heather, you always eat vegetables and fruits and all this strange stuff that looks so boring and gross. YUCK! Why don't you eat something fun like all of us? I have my cookies and chips for a snack. I don't see anyone else in this class eating like you! No one wants to play with you or eat snacks with you because you are so different!"

Many of the other kids would laugh with Billy. Healthy Heather would feel sad, but she was always kind and helpful to all of her classmates. She didn't let the teasing stop her from eating her healthy foods, always being kind, and having her superpowers.

Heather did enjoy eating cake and sweet treats on her birthday and other special occasions, but she really enjoyed eating her fruits and vegetables. She called them her "superhero foods."

However, Heather did have one special friend named Sensitive Sienna. Sienna would quietly watch Billy the Bully be unkind and tease Healthy Heather because she was different. She would say to Billy, "You are not being very nice to Heather. You eat a lot of sugar and junk food. You should try sharing her healthy snacks sometime and stop teasing her!" She would say to Heather, "Don't listen to Billy. He is mean. I think it is great that you eat all of these fruits and vegetables. I love them too! Can I have some with you?"

Every day, Heather would share her fruits and vegetables with Sensitive Sienna, and they would eat together and talk. Heather was happy to have a great friend like Sienna.

During snack time one day, Healthy Heather found out from her teacher, Mrs. Motivator, that they were going to have two very special guests visit her classroom. It was going to be two of her heroes, Olympic athletes Will the Weight Lifter and Gina the Gymnast. Her entire classroom cheered when they found out they would get to meet them!

The night before Will the Weight Lifter and Gina the Gymnast visited Heather's classroom, she was so excited she could barely sleep. She woke up the next morning and ran downstairs.

"Mom and Dad, I am so excited to meet my heroes Will and Gina today. They are so strong and healthy and happy. I really hope I can take a picture with them so I never forget this day. It would make me so happy! This is going to be the best day ever!"

When she got to school, all of her classmates were so excited. They were all laughing and giggling and waiting patiently for Will the Weight Lifter and Gina the Gymnast to arrive. As usual, the students had their morning snacks before their special guests arrived.

Today Heather had carrots and blueberries for a snack. As usual, Billy the Bully came up to her and teased her. "Heather, you really eat strange food, yuck! You eat so many fruits and vegetables. My snacks are so much better than yours."

Heather did not pay any attention to Billy the Bully today. She was too excited about Will the Weight Lifter and Gina the Gymnast coming to her classroom. As usual, Sensitive Sienna came over to Healthy Heather and asked to share her yummy healthy snacks.

After snack time, Mrs. Motivator called all of the students to sit in a circle. All of the children clapped and cheered when Will the Weight Lifter and Gina the Gymnast arrived. They talked about how hard they practiced every day to become Olympic athletes.

"Practice makes perfect. You have to work hard and focus, and you will achieve all of your goals and dreams. It is so important to read books, study and learn, exercise, get a good night's sleep, be kind to everyone, and eat healthy foods."

Billy the Bully raised his hand and said, "Will, you are my hero. I want to be an Olympic weight flifter and be big and strong like you someday!"

"Well, besides eating healthy, a big part of being successful is being kind to others."

Billy the Bully looked down at his feet because he knew he was not always nice to Healthy Heather.

Billy the Bully stood up and looked over at Healthy Heather and said to Will and Gina, "I want to say sorry to Heather. I have not always been nice to her because she is different and eats all of these weird foods like fruits and vegetables all of the time."

Billy the Bully looked at Healthy Heather and said, "I am sorry Heather, I will never tease you or anyone else again."

Heather smiled and said, "That's okay, Billy. I accept your apology!"

Gina said, "Now that is the start of a friendship and being a hero!"

"One of the things that makes each and every one of us wonderful is that we are all different! We all have different talents and ideas that make us special. We should always accept and celebrate what makes us all different. As for eating healthy, Heather eats many of the great foods that we eat as Olympic athletes."

"She does?" said Billy the Bully.

"Yes," said Will. "I was watching her during snack time today, and she had carrots and blueberries, which are so healthy. It is so important to eat as many vegetables as we can every day. They give us special vitamins that our body needs to grow big and strong and stay healthy. Fruits like blueberries have special things in them called antioxidants and phytonutrients. They give our fruits and vegetables their beautiful bright colors and keep us healthy. I can tell you that all athletes and superheroes make sure they eat their fruits and vegetables every day."

"WOW!" said Billy the Bully. "I am going to start eating my fruits and vegetables every day, too, like Heather! What else should we eat?"

"Well, you also want to make sure you are eating healthy protein every day. Protein helps us to build our muscles and stay big and strong. Some great things to eat to get protein are eggs, chicken, turkey, fish, beans, tofu, nuts, and seeds. We also get protein from dairy like milk, cheese, and yogurt."

"I eat all of those things!" Heather exclaimed.

"We also want to make sure we are eating healthy carbohydrates!"

"Carbo-what?" asked Sensitive Sienna.

"Carbohydrates! They provide our body with energy, and they are the fuel for our bodies."

"Is it like when we stop at the gas station with our parents to fill our car up with gas?" asked Heather.

"YES!" exclaimed Gymnast Gina. "That's a great example, Heather. Carbohydrates give our body the fuel we need to go, like filling a car up with gas so it can drive!"

Billy the Bully asked, "So what kinds of foods are carbohydrates?"

Will the Weight Lifter said, "There are many things, but some good things we can have are whole-wheat bread and pasta, beans, oatmeal, rice, potatoes, and whole-wheat crackers."

"Yes, I eat all of those too!" exclaimed Healthy Heather.

"There is one last thing we want to make sure we are eating every day too. It is what we call fats."

"Fats are good for us?" asked Sensitive Sienna. "I thought I heard my mommy and daddy say they were not good one time."

Gina the Gymnast said, "There are certain kinds of fats that are not good for us, like fried foods such as french fries and fried chicken. But healthy fats are like little building blocks that can help give us the energy to run and play and learn in school. They help us stay warm so we are not cold all of the time, and they help protect our hearts. Some great things we can eat to get good fats are avocados, coconuts, butter, peanut butter and almond butter, sunflower butter, and salmon."

Health Heather stood up and exclaimed, "I eat all of those too!"

Billy the Bully asked, "What about yummy stuff like cake, ice cream, and cookies?"

"Yes," said Gina, "these things taste yummy. You can enjoy these things once in a while. It is a lot of fun to share a sweet snack with friends every now and then. But these things all have added sugar, which is not very good for our health. It is not good for our teeth and can make us tired and sluggish if we eat too much."

Billy asked, "So it's okay to have an ice cream sundae or cookies with my parents and sister on the weekend, but not every day, right?"

"Exactly, Billy," said Gina.

Heather couldn't contain her excitement anymore. She ran over to her lunch box and pulled out her lunch to show Will the Weight Lifter and Gina the Gymnast. She had chicken, a slice of whole-wheat bread, sunflower butter, broccoli, apples, yogurt, and water for lunch.

"I think I have my protein and dairy, carbohydrates, fats, and fruits and vegetables all here!" she said.

"You sure do!" Will the Weight Lifter exclaimed. "Heather's lunch looks exactly like the meals Gymnast Gina and I eat every day to stay healthy and strong and have a lot of energy!"

Healthy Heather was so excited, she jumped up and down and forgot about her superpowers. She jumped so high that the top of her head touched the ceiling, and she lifted the entire bookshelf over her head out of excitement. She suddenly had muscles and was wearing a cape! All of her classmates shouted with excitement and couldn't believe it.

"Heather is a superhero! She is strong because of her healthy foods and fruits and vegetables. Yay for Heather!"

Will the Weightlifter and Gina the Gymnast could not believe how strong she was.

"Yes, she has special powers and eats very healthy. She is a great example for all of us! Although we may not all have superpowers like Heather, eating lots of fruits and vegetables will keep us healthy. They will give us the energy we need to achieve everything we want to."

Will the Weight Lifter said, "Heather, thank you for setting a wonderful example for all of your classmates and always being kind to everyone. Would you like to take a picture with Gina the Gymnast and me?"

Heather exclaimed, "Yes, I am so excited. You and Gina are my heroes! This has been the best day ever!"

After Heather took a photograph with Will the Weight Lifter and Gina the Gymnast, they invited the entire class to take a picture together.

"Let's not forget this great day together. Always be kind and loving to each other, celebrate all of our wonderful differences, eat less junk food, and don't forget to eat your fruits and vegetables!"

Made in the USA
Monee, IL
12 December 2019